PREPARING FOR CONFIRMATION

My Weekly Mass Journal

FELICIA NAVARRO

My Weekly
MASS
Journal

Preparing for *Confirmation*

TWENTY
THIRD 23rd
PUBLICATIONS

TWENTY-THIRD PUBLICATIONS
A Division of Bayard
One Montauk Avenue, Suite 200
New London, CT 06320
(860) 437-3012
(800) 321-0411
www.23rdpublications.com

Fourth printing 2014

ISBN 978-1-58595-842-9

Printed in the U.S.A.

CONTENTS

WELCOME, CONFIRMATION CANDIDATE!

As you prepare for the sacrament of confirmation, the Church is full of joy for you. At baptism, you became an heir to the kingdom of heaven. Your parents, godparents, and the whole community of believers vowed to take part in your formation. Confirmation is how *you* take part in that formation. The sacrament deepens your baptismal grace, uniting you even more firmly to Jesus Christ.

Through the full outpouring of the Holy Spirit—which was instituted by Jesus when he conferred it on the Apostles at Pentecost—your bond with Christ's Church is made more perfect. The Holy Spirit strengthens your ability to spread and defend your Catholic faith. The seven gifts of the Spirit— wisdom, understanding, counsel, fortitude, knowledge, piety, and fear of the Lord—are increased at confirmation. These gifts allow you to truly live in the fruits of the Holy Spirit: charity, joy, peace, patience, kindness, goodness, generosity, gentleness, faithfulness, modesty, chastity, and self-control.

An indelible character is imprinted on your soul at confirmation, and you will forever be counted as a member of Christ's one, holy, catholic, and apostolic Church.

This journal will help you keep track of your preparation. But there's much more here. First, as you participate in the highest form of prayer—the Mass—the study pages will help you deepen your experience of that hour you spend in church. By observing, thinking, and then completing the worksheet, you'll discover things about the Mass you may never have known before. You'll also discover things about yourself and your relationship to God. (Note that on each Mass worksheet you will find quotes from Scripture. These aren't necessarily from the Mass readings for the day, but are included to help and inspire you.)

Each worksheet page also includes either a quote from a saint in **So Say the Saints** or an **FYCI** (For Your Catholic Information), which are tidbits or helpful and meaningful facts about our Catholic faith.

The **Challenge Search Projects** will help you continue to seek out the truths and fruitfulness of your faith.

Finally, the **Service Project Self-Accountability Record** is a good starting point for you to participate in the apostolic works of the Church.

May this little booklet, along with your participation in your parish program, bring you ever deeper in love with God, your own Catholic faith and the faithful community around you.

May the Lord bless you!

CHOOSING A SPONSOR

A sponsor must be at least sixteen years old. He or she must be a Catholic who has been confirmed, is in good standing with the Church, and able to receive Holy Communion. While your sponsor cannot be your parent, he or she can be your godparent—a person who was chosen by your parents at your baptism.

WHAT DOES A SPONSOR DO?

Your sponsor is someone who will guide you in living a full Christian life. He or she should be present and available during the time of preparation and certainly at the celebration of the sacrament. On the day of confirmation, your sponsor presents you to the bishop for anointing. Later, your sponsor faithfully helps you fulfill your baptismal promises under the influence of the Holy Spirit (Canon Law 892).

CHOOSING A CONFIRMATION NAME

The Church encourages you to use the saint's name given to you at baptism as your confirmation name, to emphasize the strong connection between these two sacraments. However, you may choose a saint's name other than your baptismal name.

As you decide on your confirmation name, think of the saints and martyrs you know about. Looking at their lives, ask yourself how they were true witnesses for Christ. Who do you think is the best role model for you today?

The saint you choose should be someone who has a unique sacramental character, and who can increase your infused virtues by example. He or she can inspire you, and help you learn more about how to be a good, active Catholic. Remember that the saint you choose will be a lasting, personal, and very real friend throughout your whole Christian journey.

Mass Appeal

For Catholics, our highest form of prayer is the Mass. At Holy Communion we celebrate all that Christ has given to us in his life, death, and resurrection.

■ At the beginning of Mass we are invited to join in singing the

_____ song or Gathering hymn.

> **Clue**
> *Answers to these questions can be found in the* **Roman Missal.** *You'll find it in your church. (It's the book that contains the Mass readings, songs, and prayers.)*

■ The Mass is celebrated in two parts: the Liturgy of the _____

and the _____ of the Eucharist.

■ After reading the gospel, the priest (or deacon or guest speaker) summarizes the readings and discusses how they apply to our lives. This is known as the

_____ .

■ In a long prayer called the _____

we proclaim what we believe as Catholics.

■ The bread and wine become the _____

and _____ of Christ.

■ Which part of the Mass do you enjoy most and why?

BONUS ▸ Other than Sundays, what other days are Catholics obligated to attend Mass?

So Say the Saints...

"Holy Communion is the shortest and safest way to heaven."   ◆ *ST. PIUS X*

FYCI

If you attended Mass every day, including Sundays, for two years, you will have covered most of the New Testament and a large portion of the Old Testament (including the Psalms) in the Bible.

Books, Books, and More Books

■ List (or attach) all the books in the Old Testament and the New Testament in the Catholic Bible.

■ There are (number) _____

books in the Old Testament and

_____ books in the New Testament,

for a total of _____ in the entire

Catholic Bible.

■ What are the first five books in the Old Testament also known as?

Clue #1
Information about the books in the Bible is usually listed in the first few pages. To determine if the Bible you are using is a Catholic Bible, look for an inprimatur.

Clue #2
Bible verses are listed by the book's title and chapter followed by the verse numbers (ex. 2 Timothy 4:2).

■ What book in the Old Testament has the most chapters?

■ Name the four Gospels:

■ The works of the Apostles are listed in what book in the New Testament?

BONUS ▷ John 3:16 is a verse from the Bible commonly seen on billboards and signs at public events, like concerts and ball games. What do you think this reading means?

F Y C I *An imprimatur (Latin for "let it be printed") is a declaration by a bishop that a published work is free of doctrinal and moral error.*

Say It Like You Believe It

At Mass, Catholics say what we believe when we make our Profession of Faith. This prayer has two versions. The Nicene Creed is a longer version that we pray at Mass. The Apostles' Creed is a shorter version (*see below*). Take a close look at this prayer right now.

Write your response after each line in the space provided. It can be your immediate reaction to the words, or a deeper reflection on what they mean to you.

I believe in God, the Father almighty, creator of heaven and earth, and in Jesus Christ, his only Son, our Lord,

who was conceived by the power of the Holy Spirit and born of the Virgin Mary,

suffered under Pontius Pilate, was crucified, died, and was buried.

He descended into hell. On the third day he arose again from the dead.

He ascended into heaven, and is seated at the right hand of the Father. From there he will come to judge the living and the dead.

I believe in the Holy Spirit,

the holy catholic Church,

the communion of saints,

the forgiveness of sins,

the resurrection of the body, and life everlasting.

Amen.

F Y C I   *Amen means "I believe" (CCC 1064).*

Who Wants to Be a Saint?

- What is the process, or steps necessary, for becoming a saint?

- What special qualities do most saints have in common?

Clue *There are many different ways to find information on saints. Ask your priest, religious education director/teacher, sponsor, or family members. When in doubt, try the Internet. There are many good Catholic websites on the lives of saints. Happy searching!*

- What confirmation name have you chosen? Which saint inspired you to choose this name?

- What about this saint's earthly or heavenly life makes you want to be more like them?

FYCI

Two miracles are the minimum necessary requirements for becoming a saint. But many saints have been credited with many more. We are all called to be saints. People who live exemplary holy lives and who inspire others to do the same become part of the communion of saints even though they have not gone through the official process, or been canonized by the pope.

Mission Possible: The Church

Jesus was about thirty years old when he began his ministry. He acknowledged his call and gathered his followers—disciples. He taught them the good news from God the Father, then challenged them to continue his mission. It was through the works of the disciples—now the Apostles—that the Church began. The *Catechism of the Catholic Church* (CCC) is a detailed teaching of our faith. It is based directly on the Bible and the traditions instituted by the Apostles. It is also developed by the authority, or Magisterium—the current bishops and cardinals who are considered successors of the Apostles—of the Church.

Jesus, on behalf of God the Father, came to accomplish salvation for mankind throughout all time. This means he didn't come only to save those who lived at the same time he did, or those who came before him. He came to save the future peoples of the world, too. That means you, today.

Jesus preached the Good News, introducing us to the Kingdom of Heaven. The Kingdom is fully achieved through his Church. (CCC 763–765)

▨ How would you tell people about the Good News that Jesus spoke about?

Once Jesus finished his earthly mission, it was up to the Apostles to continue his work. The Holy Spirit came upon them at Pentecost so that the Church would always be kept holy. The Holy Spirit also makes the Church "missionary," that is, the Church makes disciples of her people—us. By faithfully observing what Jesus teaches us about charity, humility and sacrifice, the Church grows and the Kingdom of heaven is fulfilled. (CCC 767-768)

■ What are some ways you can help the Church grow?

The love Christ has for the Church is similar, yet more spectacular, to the love of a groom for his bride. The Church, being this bride, loves Jesus just the same. They are devoted to each other in perfect union. As baptized members of the Church, we grow in union with Christ and work toward the perfection of this great mystery. (CCC 773)

■ How can your relationship with Christ help strengthen the Church?

BONUS Explain how Jesus made Peter the head of the Church (Matthew 16:16-19).

Who is our current pope—the successor to Peter?

Mother Mary—Model of the Holy Way

Mary is Jesus' first and most faithful disciple. Among all women, she was chosen by God to be the mother of his Son. He exempted her from original sin, creating in her a pure heart. Because of this, she is known to us as the Immaculate Conception.

It was at Mary's insistence that Jesus performed his first miracle at the wedding feast at Cana, turning water into fine wine. She supported Jesus throughout his ministry and stood by the cross as he died. In many ways Mary is the perfect example of discipleship and she is a model for all of us. Like Mary, we need to be open to the ways God may be calling us.

We believe that when Mary's work on earth was done, God brought her—body and soul—to live forever with the risen Christ. This belief is called the Assumption. Today, Mary continues to help bring us closer to her Son.

- What are some ways you can call on Mary?

- Mary has many titles. List three you like the most:

- The rosary: How many mysteries are prayed in one rosary?

- How many Hail Marys are in one decade of the rosary?

- In what ways do you think Mary is a model of holiness?

BONUS Read John 19:26–27. Were these words meant for Saint John alone? Explain.

Decisions, Decisions...

The Ten Commandments guide us in making good decisions and help us to follow God's way. A sin is when we break, or fail to follow, the Ten Commandments. A venial sin is considered a small sin that weakens our relationship with God. Mortal sin is a big sin that separates us from God.

■ List (or attach) the Ten Commandments.

■ The first three Commandments deal directly with our

relationship to _____ .

■ The rest of the Commandments deal directly with how we

relate to _____ .

■ How can you form a good conscience? (Example: praying)

How do Catholics reconcile our sins?

BONUS What do you think the following means?

In order to reach a good end result all circumstances present must also be good. A bad act, even to produce a good end result, makes an entire act wrong.

> "Every moral act consists of three elements: the objective act (what we do), the subjective goal or intention (why we do the act), and the concrete situation or circumstances in which we perform the act....All three aspects must be good... in order to have a morally good act." (*United States Catholic Catechism for Adults*, U.S. Conference of Catholic Bishops, July 2006, p. 311–312).

FYCI

Concupiscence is the human inclination or desire to act outside of God's will as a result of original sin. Baptism does not clear us of this inclination. This means that we have to rely on our faith, conscience and intellect as well as God's Grace to make good decisions. (CCC 1264)

Rules of Engagement

THE PRECEPTS OF THE CHURCH

In order to grow in love of God and neighbor we must be committed to prayer and moral actions nourished by a liturgical life, therefore...

1. You shall go to Mass on Sundays—the day of Jesus' resurrection—and holy days of obligation. You shall also rest from work on these days.

2. You shall confess your sins at least once a year in the Sacrament of Reconciliation.

3. You shall receive the sacrament of the Eucharist (Holy Communion) at least once during the Easter Season.

4. You shall observe the days of fasting and abstinence established by the Church.

5. You shall help to provide for the needs of the Church by sharing your treasures, your time and your talents. (CCC 2041-43)

By following the Precepts of the Church we grow closer to God and his Church and are able to spread the Good News of Christ to all peoples.

■ We attend _____ on _____ ,

because it is the Lord's Day, the day he rose from the dead. We

also _____ on this day.

■ Every Catholic should participate in the Sacrament of _____ at least once during the year.

■ We should receive _____ frequently, preferably every time we participate in the Eucharist, provided we are free from mortal sin, but we should definitely receive during _____ Season.

■ _____ means eating a lesser amount of food as a sacrifice, especially on Ash Wednesday and Good Friday.

■ The faithful have a duty to support the needs of the _____ .

■ Someone who enjoys singing can share their _____ by cantoring at Mass.

■ We can each carry on the work of Christ by spreading the _____ far and wide.

BONUS Think about the many ways God has blessed you with unique talents. How can you continue to serve the Church with your talents?

Confirm Me—Ready, Willing, and Able

For many of us, our parents brought us to God at baptism. For the next few years they taught us about God, the Catholic faith, and the Church.

The full outpouring of the Spirit and the completion of baptismal grace occurs at confirmation. This is your personal commitment to God. It is also God's acceptance of your promise to love and protect the Church, and to continue growing in faith, knowledge, and prayer. The laying on of hands and anointing with chrism (holy oil) is an invitation to the Holy Spirit by the bishop, the assembly and the confirmand (that's you), to once again come upon you. This time, the Spirit is asked to seal you with his gifts. Now you take on a new role in the Church.

Many people find one of the greatest challenges after confirmation is understanding their role as confirmed Catholics. Some of us think we are finished, as if confirmation is like a graduation. But this sacrament is the beginning of our personal journey with God and his Church. When we accept the Gift of the Holy Spirit, we acknowledge the need for God in our lives. We promise to nourish and build on this relationship.

In fact, we always have much to learn about our faith. There are things you will learn years from now, because the Church is full of beauty and wonder. To know it all now would be too much for anyone to take in all at once. Over 2000 years, the Church has developed a rich culture and way of life. You will find prayers that have deeper meanings for you at various places in your life journey. You will encounter hundreds of saints who can help you at different times. You can read many rewarding and insightful books. The Holy Spirit helps all of us learn and seek out our faith at all times and in all ways.

■ How can you continue to learn and grow in your faith once you are confirmed?

■ Find a new prayer you have never learned and pray it. Write about how it made you feel and how it helped you grow closer to God. Write the title of this prayer here:

BONUS How do you think you are ready, willing, and able to be confirmed in your faith?

Presents! I Like Presents!

The Seven Gifts of the Holy Spirit are outpoured in the sacrament of confirmation. At baptism we receive the Holy Spirit, but the gifts are shared with us by our parents, teachers, priests, religious, and others who are part of our Catholic upbringing. They instruct and teach us about God, Jesus, and the Church. They also teach us how to apply the Good News of Christ into our own lives. The Holy Spirit gives us these gifts at confirmation so we can grow in our own faith and share all that we have learned and experienced with others.

Challenge yourself to do the following project: Gather seven small boxes. (Jewelry boxes work well. You can also use blank envelopes.) Write the name of each gift of the Holy Spirit on separate index cards. On the back of each card, answer the question (below) about the gift. Place each card in a separate box or envelope. If you use boxes, wrap them with gift wrap. Do not label them. Beginning seven days before your confirmation, open one box or envelope each night. Open the last one on the morning of this great celebration. Keep these "gifts" as reminders of your confirmation preparation experience.

WISDOM A gift of knowing and doing good. It's about sharing good advice and knowing when someone gives you good advice. This gift helps you see God in your actions and your words.

■ Who in your life inspires you to embrace this gift by how they have shared this gift with you? How have they shared this gift?

UNDERSTANDING This is more than comprehension. It is a gift of compassion, too. Compassion is the gift that allows you to share God with those who need to know and love him more.

▨ When you needed to be understood and loved, who helped you experience it, and how?

COUNSEL This is the gift of right judgment. With this gift you are able to make decisions that are not only good for you, but good for the people around you, too.

▨ Write about a situation at home, school, church, or in your community in which someone did something to benefit others. How does this inspire you to make good choices for yourself and others?

FORTITUDE A gift of courage. This gift helps you stand up for your faith and other things you believe in. With this gift you can overcome obstacles.

▨ Who is the most courageous person you know? How can you learn to be more like them?

KNOWLEDGE This gift sounds like wisdom and understanding, but it is a gift of learning. By being open to God and all that he wants you to know about him, you grow in your relationships with family, friends, God, and the world around you.

▓ What are some ways that you can commit to learning more about God and the Church?

PIETY This gift gives you confidence in God and in the love he has for you. It inspires you to love him back and share his love with others.

▓ Who has shared God's love with you, and how will you share his love with others?

WONDER AND AWE *(also known as Fear of the Lord)* This gift is a desire for God and his immeasurable love in your life. With this gift you know just how much you want to grow in your love for God.

▓ What are some ways that you would like to grow in your love for God? How can you achieve that every day of your life from this moment on?

Calendar Date: _____

Church Calendar Date: _____

(i.e., 27th Sunday in Ordinary Time, Feast of Christ the King, Christmas Eve)

After Jesus was baptized, he came up from the water and behold, the heavens were opened (for him), and he saw the Spirit of God descending like a dove (and) coming upon him. And a voice came from the heavens, saying, "This is my beloved Son, with whom I am well pleased." MATTHEW 3:16-17

Which Mass did you attend today? *(Time and parish)*

St. Mary's   11:00 mass

Who was the main celebrant or presider? *(Name of priest who led the celebration of the Mass)*

What in particular do you remember about Mass? *(Think about the vestment colors, readings, songs, or something said during the homily)*

What did Jesus say or do in the Gospel reading?

What about Jesus' words or actions makes you want to follow him more closely?

So Say the Saints...

"Love consumes us only in the measure of our self-surrender."   ◆ *ST. THERESE OF LISIEUX*

23

Calendar Date: _____

Church Calendar Date: _____

(i.e., 27th Sunday in Ordinary Time, Feast of Christ the King, Christmas Eve)

...The fruit of the Spirit is love, joy, peace, patience, kindness, generosity, faithfulness, gentleness, self control. Against such there is no law.   GALATIANS 5:22-23

What was today's Gospel reading? *(Cite book, chapter, and verses)*

Isahia

How did the Homily relate to today's readings?

During the Eucharistic Prayer we give thanks and praise to God. What are you grateful for today?

How did the songs relate to the different parts of the Mass?
(Example: Communion song was about the Body of Christ.)

The Entrance song was about:

The song at the Presentation of the Gifts was about:

The Communion song was about:

The Dismissal song was about:

So Say the Saints...

"To love God is something greater than to know him."
◆ *ST. THOMAS AQUINAS*

24

Calendar Date: _____

Church Calendar Date: _____

(i.e., 27th Sunday in Ordinary Time, Feast of Christ the King, Christmas Eve)

For however many are the promises of God, their Yes is in him; therefore, the Amen from us also goes through him to God for glory. But the one who gives us security with you in Christ and who anointed us is God; he has also put his seal upon us and given the Spirit in our hearts as a first installment. 2 CORINTHIANS 1:20–22

Which Mass did you attend today? *(Time and parish)*

Other than the priest, who else processed in during the Entrance song?

Did they carry anything? What was it?

Which reading from today, including the Psalm Response, could you relate to most, and why?

How did the Homily relate to things going on in your life? *(At home, at school, with friends, in the world, in your local community, at your church)*

So Say the Saints...

"Grant me, O Lord my God, a mind to know you, a heart to seek you, wisdom to find you, conduct pleasing to you, faithful perseverance in waiting for you, and a hope of finally embracing you." ◆ *ST. THOMAS AQUINAS*

Calendar Date: _____

Church Calendar Date: _____
(i.e., 27th Sunday in Ordinary Time, Feast of Christ the King, Christmas Eve)

> "Ah, Lord God!" I said, "I know not how to speak; I am too young."
> But the Lord answered me, "Say not, 'I am too young.' To whomever
> I send you, you shall go; whatever I command you, you shall speak.
> Have no fear before them, because I am with you to deliver you, says
> the Lord." Then the Lord extended his hand and touched my mouth,
> saying, "See, I place my words in your mouth!"   JEREMIAH 1:6-9

What was today's Psalm Response? In what ways can this help
you during the week?

What was today's Gospel reading? *(Cite book, chapter, and verses)*

During the readings, including the Psalm Response, what person
or thing can you identify with, and why?

What was the Recessional hymn or Closing song, and what was
it about?

So Say the Saints...

"Fall, fall in love with God, and let your soul and
conscience grow big in him! Don't chose to do the bare
minimum, for that cuts off the arms of holy desire."
♦ *ST. CATHERINE OF SIENA*

Calendar Date: _____

Church Calendar Date: _____

(i.e., 27th Sunday in Ordinary Time, Feast of Christ the King, Christmas Eve)

For so the Lord has commanded us, "I have made you a light to the Gentiles, that you may be an instrument of salvation to the ends of the earth." The Gentiles were delighted when they heard this and glorified the word of the Lord. All who were destined for eternal life came to believe, and the word of the Lord continued to spread through the whole region. ACTS 13:47–49

What were today's first and second readings? *(Cite books, chapters, and verses)*

During the Gloria we give praise to God. In what ways will you praise God this week?

In the Prayer of the Faithful, we pray specifically for our Church and her leaders, for leaders of nations and local governments, for people in need, and for things in our own families. What special intentions do you and your family have for today?

In the Gospel reading, what did Jesus say or do?

How did it change the story?

How can this story from the Gospel relate to your own life?

So Say the Saints...

"May your creed be for you as a mirror. Look at yourself in it, to see if you believe everything you say you believe. And rejoice in your faith each day." ● *ST. AUGUSTINE*

27

Calendar Date: _____

Church Calendar Date: _____

(i.e., 27th Sunday in Ordinary Time, Feast of Christ the King, Christmas Eve)

> But when he comes, the Spirit of truth, he will guide you to all truth. He will not speak on his own, but he will speak what he hears, and will declare to you the things that are coming. He will glorify me, because he will take from what is mine and declare it to you.
>
> JOHN 16:13-14

What was today's Gospel about? How did the people respond to Jesus?

How would you respond to him?

What do you remember about church today? *(Think about things like the windows, the colors, or the vestments)*

During the Offertory, gifts are presented at the altar. What special gifts will you offer this week at home, church or school?

Mass concludes with a special blessing from the priest so we can glorify the Lord by our lives. In what ways were you able to do that last week?

So Say the Saints...

"My longing for truth was a single prayer."   ◆ *EDITH STEIN*

Calendar Date: _____

Church Calendar Date: _____

(i.e., 27th Sunday in Ordinary Time, Feast of Christ the King, Christmas Eve)

The Spirit of the Lord is upon me, because he has anointed me to bring glad tidings to the poor. He has sent me to proclaim liberty to captives and recovery of sight to the blind, to let the oppressed go free, and to proclaim a year acceptable to the Lord. LUKE 4:18-19

Which Mass did you attend today? *(Time and parish)*

Who was the main celebrant, or presider? *(Name of priest who led the celebration of the Mass)*

What in particular do you remember about Mass today? *(Think about the vestment colors, readings, songs, something said during the homily)*

What did Jesus say or do in the Gospel reading today?

What about his words or actions makes you want to follow him more closely?

So Say the Saints...

"The proof of love is in the works. Where love exists, it works great things. But when it ceases to act, it ceases to exist." ◆ *ST. GREGORY THE GREAT*

Calendar Date: _____

Church Calendar Date: _____
(i.e., 27th Sunday in Ordinary Time, Feast of Christ the King, Christmas Eve)

God raised this Jesus; of this we are all witnesses. Exalted at the right hand of God, he received the promise of the Holy Spirit from the Father and poured it forth, as you (both) see and hear.   ACTS 2:32-33

What was today's Gospel reading? *(Cite book, chapter, and verses)*

How did the Homily relate to today's readings?

During the Eucharistic Prayer we give thanks and praise to God. What are you grateful for today?

How did the songs relate to the different parts of the Mass? *(Example: Communion song was about the Body of Christ.)*

The Entrance song was about:

The song at the Presentation of the Gifts was about:

The Communion song was about:

The Dismissal song was about:

F Y C I   *When Jesus was on the cross and said, "My God, my God, why have you forsaken me?" he was actually praying the 22nd Psalm. Jesus knew the psalms by heart and prayed them regularly. Psalm 22 is about deliverance from suffering.*

Calendar Date: _____

Church Calendar Date: _____

(i.e., 27th Sunday in Ordinary Time, Feast of Christ the King, Christmas Eve)

> *For I, the Lord, love what is right, I hate robbery and injustice; I will give them their recompense faithfully, a lasting covenant I will make with them.* ISAIAH 61:8

Which Mass did you attend today? *(Time and parish)*

Other than the priest, who else processed in during the Entrance song?

Did they carry anything? What was it?

Which reading from today, including the Psalm Response, could you relate to most, and why?

How did the Homily relate to things going on in your life? *(At home, at school, with friends, in the world, in your local community, at your church)*

So Say the Saints...

"Virtues are formed by prayer. Prayer preserves temperance. Prayer suppresses anger. Prayer prevents emotions of pride and envy. Prayer draws into the soul the Holy Spirit, and raises man to heaven." ◆ *ST. EPHRAEM*

31

Calendar Date: _____

Church Calendar Date: _____
(i.e., 27th Sunday in Ordinary Time, Feast of Christ the King, Christmas Eve)

Now you are Christ's body, and individually parts of it. Some people God has designated in the church to be, first, apostles; second, prophets; third, teachers; then, mighty deeds; then, gifts of healing, assistance, administration, and varieties of tongues.

1 CORINTHIANS 12:27-28

What was today's Psalm Response?

In what ways can the Psalm Response help you during the week?

What was today's Gospel reading? *(Cite book, chapter, and verses)*

During the readings, including the Psalm Response, what person or thing could you identify with and why?

What was the Recessional hymn or Closing song, and what was it about?

F Y C I

The Eucharist, which means "thanksgiving" in Greek, is the Body of Christ, in the appearance of bread. As members of the Catholic faith, we share in the celebration of the Eucharist at Mass.

Calendar Date: _____

Church Calendar Date: _____

(i.e., 27th Sunday in Ordinary Time, Feast of Christ the King, Christmas Eve)

If the Spirit of the one who raised Jesus from the dead dwells in you, the one who raised Christ from the dead will give life to your mortal bodies also, through his Spirit that dwells in you. ROMANS 8:11

What were today's first and second readings? *(Cite books, chapters, and verses)*

During the Gloria we give praise to God. In what ways will you praise God this week?

In the Prayer of the Faithful we pray specifically for our Church and her leaders, for leaders of nations and local governments, for people in need, and for things in our own families. What special intentions do you and your family have for today?

During the Gospel reading what did Jesus say or do?

How did it change the story?

How can this story from the Gospel relate to your own life?

F
Y
C
I
Consecration is the moment during Mass when the bread and wine become the Body and Blood of Christ. It happens in the second part of the Mass—the Liturgy of the Eucharist.

33

Calendar Date: _____

Church Calendar Date: _____

(i.e., 27th Sunday in Ordinary Time, Feast of Christ the King, Christmas Eve)

What has happened all over Judea, beginning in Galilee after the baptism that John preached, how God anointed Jesus of Nazareth with the Holy Spirit and power. He went about doing good and healing all those oppressed by the devil, for God was with him.
ACTS 10:37-38

What was today's Gospel about?

How did the people respond to Jesus?

How would you respond to him?

What do you remember about church today? *(Think about things like the windows, the colors, or the vestments)*

During the Offertory, gifts are presented at the altar. What special gifts will you offer this week at home, church or school?

Mass concludes with a special blessing from the priest so that we can glorify the Lord by our lives. In what ways were you able to do that last week?

F Y C I
The word "liturgy" originally meant a "public work," or a "service in the name of, or on behalf of the people." In Christian tradition it means the participation of the people of God in "the work of God" (CCC 1069).

Calendar Date: _____

Church Calendar Date: _____

(i.e., 27th Sunday in Ordinary Time, Feast of Christ the King, Christmas Eve)

"When the Advocate comes whom I will send you from the Father, the Spirit of truth that proceeds from the Father, he will testify to me. And you also testify, because you have been with me from the beginning." JOHN 15:26-27

Which Mass did you attend today? *(Time and parish)*

Who was the main celebrant or presider? *(Name of priest who led the celebration of the Mass)*

What in particular do you remember about Mass? *(Think about the vestment colors, readings, songs, or something said during the homily)*

What did Jesus say or do in the Gospel reading?

What about his words or actions makes you want to follow him more closely?

**F
Y
C
I** *At confirmation the bishop says, "(Your confirmation name), be sealed with the Gift of the Holy Spirit." This gift is not referring to the seven Gifts of the Spirit. The Holy Spirit is the Gift.*

35

(i.e., 27th Sunday in Ordinary Time, Feast of Christ the King, Christmas Eve)

> *And the angel said to her in reply, "The Holy Spirit will come upon you, and the power of the Most High will overshadow you. Therefore the child to be born will be called holy, the Son of God. And behold, Elizabeth, your relative, has also conceived a son in her old age, and this is the sixth month for her who was called barren; for nothing will be impossible for God."* LUKE 1:35-37

What was today's Gospel reading? *(Cite book, chapter, and verses)*

How did the Homily relate to today's readings?

During the Eucharistic Prayer we give thanks and praise to God. What are you grateful for today?

How did the songs sung at Mass today relate to the different parts of the Mass? *(Example: Communion song was about the Body of Christ)*

The Entrance song was about:

The song at the Presentation of the Gifts was about:

The Communion song was about:

The Dismissal song was about:

F
Y
C
I

The Feast of the Immaculate Conception is December 8. Many people think this is about Jesus, but in fact Mary, the Mother of Jesus, is the Immaculate Conception—this means she was chosen by God before she was even conceived.

Church Calendar Date: _____

(i.e., 27th Sunday in Ordinary Time, Feast of Christ the King, Christmas Eve)

It happened in those days that Jesus came from Nazareth of Galilee and was baptized in the Jordan by John. On coming up out of the water he saw the heavens being torn open and the Spirit, like a dove, descending upon him.   MARK 1:9-10

Which Mass did you attend today? *(Time and parish)*

Other than the priest, who else processed in during the Entrance song?

Did they carry anything? What was it?

Which reading, including the Psalm Response, could you relate to most, and why?

How did the Homily relate to things going on in your life? *(At home, at school, with friends, in the world, in your local community, at your church)*

So Say the Saints...

"Nothing is far from God."   ◆ *ST. MONICA*

Calendar Date: _____

Church Calendar Date: _____

           (i.e., 27th Sunday in Ordinary Time, Feast of Christ the King, Christmas Eve)

> *Behold, my servant whom I have chosen, my beloved in whom I delight; I shall place my spirit upon him, and he will proclaim justice to the Gentiles. He will not contend or cry out, nor will anyone hear his voice in the streets. A bruised reed he will not break, a smoldering wick he will not quench, until he brings justice to victory. And in his name the Gentiles will hope.*   MATTHEW 12:18-21

What was today's Psalm Response?

In what ways can this help you during the week?

What was today's Gospel reading? *(Cite book, chapter, and verses)*

During the readings, including the Psalm Response, what person or thing could you identify with, and why?

What was the Recessional hymn or Closing song, and what was it about?

So Say the Saints...

"The first end I propose in our daily work is to do the will of God; secondly, to do it in the manner he wills it; and thirdly, to do it because it is his will."

   ◆ *ST. ELIZABETH ANN SETON*

Calendar Date: _____

Church Calendar Date: _____

(i.e., 27th Sunday in Ordinary Time, Feast of Christ the King, Christmas Eve)

> *On that day you will realize that I am in my Father and you are in me and I in you. Whoever has my commandments and observes them is the one who loves me. And whoever loves me will be loved by my Father, and I will love him and reveal myself to him.* JOHN 14:20-21

What were today's first and second readings? *(Cite books, chapters, and verses)*

During the Gloria we give praise to God. In what ways will you praise God this week?

In the Prayer of the Faithful we pray specifically for our Church and her leaders, for leaders of nations and local governments, for people in need, and for things in our own families. What special intentions do you and your family have for today?

In the Gospel reading what did Jesus say or do?

How did it change the story?

How can this story from the Gospel relate to your own life?

So Say the Saints...

"Love God, serve God: everything is in that."

◆ *ST. CLARE OF ASSISI*

Calendar Date: _____

Church Calendar Date: _____

(i.e., 27th Sunday in Ordinary Time, Feast of Christ the King, Christmas Eve)

But you will receive power when the Holy Spirit comes upon you, and you will be my witnesses in Jerusalem, throughout Judea and Samaria, and to the ends of the earth. ACTS 1:8

What was today's Gospel about?

How did the people respond to Jesus?

How would you respond to Jesus?

What do you remember about church today? (*Think about things like the windows, the colors, or the vestments*)

During the Offertory, gifts are presented at the altar. What special gifts will you offer this week at home, church or school?

Mass concludes with a special blessing from the priest so that we can glorify the Lord by our lives. In what ways were you able to do that last week?

So Say the Saints...

"Those whose hearts are pure are temples of the Holy Spirit." ◆ *ST. LUCY*

Calendar Date: _____

Church Calendar Date: _____

(i.e., 27th Sunday in Ordinary Time, Feast of Christ the King, Christmas Eve)

> Now when the apostles in Jerusalem heard that Samaria had accepted the word of God, they sent them Peter and John, who went down and prayed for them, that they might receive the Holy Spirit, for it had not yet fallen upon any of them; they had only been baptized in the name of the Lord Jesus. Then they laid hands on them and they received the Holy Spirit.   ACTS 8:14-17

Which Mass did you attend today? *(Time and parish)*

Who was the main celebrant or presider? *(Name of priest who led the celebration of the Mass)*

What in particular do you remember about Mass? *(Think about the vestment colors, readings, songs, something said during the homily)*

What did Jesus say or do in the Gospel reading?

What about his words or actions makes you want to follow him more closely?

F Y C I

Mary's apparition in Tepeyac, Mexico to Saint Juan Diego, and the miraculous image of her imprinted on his tilma (poncho), is credited for converting over four million Mexican Native Indians. Our Lady of Guadalupe is the patroness of the Americas.

Calendar Date: _____

Church Calendar Date: _____

(i.e., 27th Sunday in Ordinary Time, Feast of Christ the King, Christmas Eve)

As I began to speak, the Holy Spirit fell upon them as it had upon us at the beginning, and I remembered the word of the Lord, how he had said, "John baptized with water but you will be baptized with the Holy Spirit." If then God gave them the same gift he gave to us when we came to believe in the Lord Jesus Christ, who was I to be able to hinder God? When they heard this, they stopped objecting and glorified God, saying, "God has then granted life-giving repentance to the Gentiles too." ACTS 11:15-18

What was today's Gospel reading? *(Cite book, chapter, and verses)*

How did the Homily relate to today's readings?

During the Eucharistic Prayer we give thanks and praise to God. What are you grateful for today?

How did the songs relate to the different parts of the Mass?
(Example: Communion song was about the Body of Christ.)

The Entrance song was about:

The song at the Presentation of the Gifts was about:

The Communion song was about:

The Dismissal song was about:

So Say the Saints...

"It is not the actual physical exertion that counts toward a man's progress, nor the nature of the task, but the spirit of faith with which it is undertaken."

◆ *ST. FRANCIS XAVIER*

Calendar Date: _____

Church Calendar Date: _____

       (i.e., 27th Sunday in Ordinary Time, Feast of Christ the King, Christmas Eve)

"The disciples were filled with joy and the Holy Spirit. ACTS 13:52

Which Mass did you attend today? *(Time and parish)*

Other than the priest, who processed in during the Entrance song?

Did they carry anything? What was it?

Which reading, including the Psalm Response, could you relate to most, and why?

How did the Homily relate to things going on in your life? *(At home, at school, with friends, in the world, in your community, at your church)*

FYCI
The first Sunday of Advent begins our Catholic calendar year. So technically, this is our New Year. This generally falls on the Sunday after the American Thanksgiving day holiday.

Calendar Date: _____

Church Calendar Date: _____

(i.e., 27th Sunday in Ordinary Time, Feast of Christ the King, Christmas Eve)

I rejoice heartily in the Lord, in my God is the joy of my soul; for he has clothed me with a robe of salvation, and wrapped me in a mantle of justice. Like a bridegroom adorned with a diadem, like a bride bedecked with her jewels. As the earth brings forth its plants, and a garden makes its growth spring up, so will the Lord God make justice and praise spring up before all the nations. ISAIAH 61:10-11

What was today's Psalm Response?

In what ways can this help you during the week?

What was today's Gospel reading? *(Cite book, chapter, and verses)*

During the readings, including the Psalm Response, what person or thing could you identify with and why?

What was the Recessional hymn or Closing song, and what was it about?

So Say the Saints...

"Who except God can give you peace? Has the world ever been able to satisfy the heart?"

◆ *ST. GERARD MAJELLA*

46

Calendar Date: _____

Church Calendar Date: _____
(i.e., 27th Sunday in Ordinary Time, Feast of Christ the King, Christmas Eve)

There are different kinds of spiritual gifts but the same Spirit; there are different forms of service but the same Lord; there are different workings but the same God who produces all of them in everyone. To each individual the manifestation of the Spirit is given for some benefit. 1 CORINTHIANS 12:4-7

What were today's first and second readings? *(Cite books, chapters, and verses)*

During the Gloria we give praise to God. In what ways will you praise God this week?

In the Prayer of the Faithful we pray specifically for our Church and her leaders, for leaders of nations and local governments, for people in need, and for things in our own families. What special intentions do you and your family have for today?

During the Gospel reading, what did Jesus say or do?

47

How did it change the story?

How can this story from the Gospel relate to your own life?

F
Y
C
I

Throughout the year in the Catholic calendar, we celebrate
the feast days of the many saints who lived exemplary lives
and who today serve as aids in prayer. Praying to saints for
their intercession is like asking a friend for a favor. Saint
Anthony has been credited with helping people find lost
items. His feast day is June 13.

Calendar Date: _____

Church Calendar Date: _____

(i.e., 27th Sunday in Ordinary Time, Feast of Christ the King, Christmas Eve)

> *The church throughout all Judea, Galilee, and Samaria was at peace. It was being built up and walked in the fear of the Lord, and with the consolation of the Holy Spirit it grew in numbers.* ACTS 9:31

Which Mass did you attend today? *(Time and parish)*

Who was the main celebrant or presider? *(Name of priest who led the celebration of the Mass)*

What in particular do you remember about Mass? *(Think about the vestment colors, readings, songs, or something said during the homily)*

What did Jesus say or do in the Gospel reading today?

What about his words or actions makes you want to follow him more closely?

F Y C I

The four marks, or identifying characteristics, of the Church are: one, holy, catholic and apostolic. The Church is instituted by the one God, through Jesus Christ. She is made holy by the Holy Spirit, her guide. The Church is also catholic in the sense that she is universal—she welcomes all people. The Church is apostolic because we trace our beginnings to Jesus' own apostles.

Calendar Date: _____

Church Calendar Date: _____
(i.e., 27th Sunday in Ordinary Time, Feast of Christ the King, Christmas Eve)

I have told you this while I am with you. The Advocate, the Holy Spirit that the Father will send in my name—he will teach you everything and remind you of all that (I) told you. Peace I leave with you; my peace I give to you. Not as the world gives do I give it to you. Do not let your hearts be troubled or afraid.   JOHN 14:25-27

What was today's Gospel reading? *(Cite book, chapter, and verses)*

How did the Homily relate to today's readings?

During the Eucharistic Prayer we give thanks and praise to God. What are you grateful for today?

How did the songs relate to the different parts of the Mass?
(Example: Communion song was about the Body of Christ.)

The Entrance song was about:

The song at the Presentation of the Gifts was about:

The Communion song was about:

F Y C I *Sundays are not counted as part of the forty days of Lent, because Sunday is a feast day of the church. This means that on Sundays you can have almost anything you give up during Lent. On this day we rest and celebrate.*

Calendar Date: _____

Church Calendar Date: _____
    (i.e., 27th Sunday in Ordinary Time, Feast of Christ the King, Christmas Eve)

> *Here is my servant whom I uphold, my chosen one with whom I am pleased, upon whom I have put my spirit; he shall bring forth justice to the nations...* ISAIAH 42:1

Which Mass did you attend today? *(Time and parish)*

Other than the priest, who else processed in during the Entrance song? Did they carry anything? What was it?

Which reading from today, including the Psalm Response, could you relate to most, and why?

How did the Homily relate to things going on in your life? *(At home, at school, with friends, in the world, in your community, at church)*

**F
Y
C
I**

Transubstantiation—*a fancy big word that will probably not show up on the SATs, but is part of the greatest miracle and mystery of our faith. Without changing their appearance, the bread and wine become the Body and Blood of Christ at the consecration of the Eucharist.*

Calendar Date: _____

Church Calendar Date: _____
(i.e., 27th Sunday in Ordinary Time, Feast of Christ the King, Christmas Eve)

Jesus answered, "Amen, amen, I say to you, no one can enter the kingdom of God without being born of water and Spirit. What is born of flesh is flesh and what is born of spirit is spirit." JOHN 3:5-6

What was today's Psalm Response?

In what ways can this help you during the week?

What was today's Gospel reading? *(Cite book, chapter, and verses)*

During the readings, including the Psalm Response, what person or thing could you identify with, and why?

What was the Recessional hymn or Closing song, and what was it about?

So Say the Saints...

"You cannot please both God and the world at the same time. They are utterly opposed to each other in their thoughts, their desires, and their actions."

◆ *ST. JOHN VIANNEY*

Calendar Date: _____

Church Calendar Date: _____

> *I am baptizing you with water, for repentance, but the one who is coming after me is mightier than I. I am not worthy to carry his sandals. He will baptize you with the Holy Spirit and fire.*
> MATTHEW 3:11

What were today's first and second readings? *(Cite books, chapters, and verses)*

During the Gloria we give praise to God. In what ways will you praise God this week?

In the Prayer of the Faithful we pray specifically for our Church and her leaders, for leaders of nations and local governments, for people in need, and for things in our own families. What special intentions do you and your family have for today?

In the Gospel reading, what did Jesus say or do?

How did it change the story?

How can this story from the Gospel relate to your own life?

So Say the Saints...

"Do not think that love, in order to be genuine, has to be extraordinary. What we need is to love without getting tired." ◆ *BL. MOTHER TERESA OF CALCUTTA*

Calendar Date: _____

Church Calendar Date: _____

(i.e., 27th Sunday in Ordinary Time, Feast of Christ the King, Christmas Eve)

"Nevertheless, do not rejoice because the spirits are subject to you, but rejoice because your names are written in heaven." At that very moment he rejoiced (in) the Holy Spirit and said, "I give you praise, Father, Lord of heaven and earth, for although you have hidden these things from the wise and the learned you have revealed them to the childlike. Yes, Father, such has been your gracious will." LUKE 10:20-21

What was today's Gospel about?

How did the people respond to Jesus?

How would you respond to him?

What do you remember about church today? *(Think about things like the windows, the colors, or the vestments)*

During the Offertory, gifts are presented at the altar. What special gifts will you offer this week at home, church, or in school?

Mass is concluded with a special blessing from the priest in order that we can glorify the Lord by our lives. In what ways were you able to do that last week?

So Say the Saints...

"If angels could be jealous of men, they would be so for one reason: Holy Communion." ◆ *ST. MAXIMILIAN KOLBE*

Calendar Date: _____

Church Calendar Date: _____

> *(i.e., 27th Sunday in Ordinary Time, Feast of Christ the King, Christmas Eve)*

> *"Then Peter proceeded to speak and said, "In truth, I see that God shows no partiality. Rather, in every nation whoever fears him and acts uprightly is acceptable to him."* ACTS 10:34-35

Which Mass did you attend today? *(Time and parish)*

Who was the main celebrant or presider? *(Name of priest who led the celebration of the Mass)*

What in particular do you remember about Mass today? *(Think about the vestment colors, readings, songs, or something said during the homily)*

What did Jesus say or do in the Gospel reading today?

What about his words or actions makes you want to follow him more closely?

So Say the Saints...

"O Holy Spirit, descend plentifully into my heart.
Enlighten the dark corners of this neglected dwelling
and scatter there thy cheerful beams." ♦ *ST. AUGUSTINE*

Calendar Date: _____

Church Calendar Date: _____

(i.e., 27th Sunday in Ordinary Time, Feast of Christ the King, Christmas Eve)

> And this is what he proclaimed: "One mightier than I is coming after me. I am not worthy to stoop and loosen the thongs of his sandals. I have baptized you with water; he will baptize you with the Holy Spirit." MARK 1:7-8

What was today's Gospel reading? (Cite book, chapter, and verses)

How did the Homily relate to today's readings?

During the Eucharistic Prayer we give thanks and praise to God. What are you grateful for today?

How did the songs relate to the different parts of the Mass? (Example: Communion song was about the Body of Christ.)

The Entrance song was about:

The song at the Presentation of the Gifts was about:

The Communion song was about:

The Dismissal song was about:

F Y C I

Certain feast days are Holy Days of Obligation and often fall during the week. December 8 and January 1 are examples of holy days that celebrate the gift God gives us in Mary, the mother of Jesus. We must go to Mass on these days.

Calendar Date: _____

Church Calendar Date: _____
(i.e., 27th Sunday in Ordinary Time, Feast of Christ the King, Christmas Eve)

God exalted him at his right hand as leader and savior to grant Israel repentance and forgiveness of sins. We are witnesses of these things, as is the Holy Spirit that God has given to those who obey him. ACTS 5:31-32

Which Mass did you attend today? *(Time and parish)*

Other than the priest, who else processed in during the Entrance song?

Did they carry anything? What was it?

Which reading from today, including the Psalm Response, could you relate to most, and why?

How did the Homily relate to things going on in your life? *(At home, at school, with friends, in the world or your community, at church)*

So Say the Saints...

"Our wish, our object, our chief preoccupation must be to form Jesus in ourselves, to make his spirit, his devotion, his affections, his desire, and his disposition live and reign there." ◆ *ST. JOHN EUDES*

Calendar Date: _____

Church Calendar Date: _____
(i.e., 27th Sunday in Ordinary Time, Feast of Christ the King, Christmas Eve)

For those who are led by the Spirit of God are children of God.
ROMANS 8:14

What was today's Psalm Response?

In what ways can this help you during the week?

What was today's Gospel reading? *(Cite book, chapter, and verses)*

During the readings, including the Psalm Response, what person or thing can you identify with, and why?

What was the Recessional hymn or Closing song, and what was it about?

F
Y
C
I

Most venial sins are forgiven during the Penitential Act (Confiteor) at Mass. That's the prayer in the beginning of Mass that begins "I confess to almighty God..."

Calendar Date: _____

Church Calendar Date: _____

(i.e., 27th Sunday in Ordinary Time, Feast of Christ the King, Christmas Eve)

Thus says God, the Lord, who created the heavens and stretched them out, who spreads out the earth with its crops, Who gives breath to its people and spirit to those who walk on it: "I, the Lord, have called you for the victory of justice, I have grasped you by the hand; I formed you, and set you as a covenant of the people, a light for the nations..." ISAIAH 42:5-6

What were today's first and second readings? *(Cite books, chapters, and verses)*

During the Gloria we give praise to God. In what ways will you praise God this week?

In the Prayer of the Faithful we pray specifically for our Church and her leaders, for leaders of nations and local governments, for people in need, and for things in our own families. What special intentions do you and your family have for today?

During the Gospel reading what did Jesus say or do?

How did it change the story?

How can this story from the Gospel relate to your own life?

So Say the Saints...

"God loves each of us as if there were only one of us."
   ◆ *ST. AUGUSTINE*

Calendar Date: _____

Church Calendar Date: _____

(i.e., 27th Sunday in Ordinary Time, Feast of Christ the King, Christmas Eve)

...The Spirit too comes to the aid of our weakness; for we do not know how to pray as we ought, but the Spirit itself intercedes with inexpressible groanings. ROMANS 8:26

What was today's Gospel about?

How did the people respond to Jesus?

How would you respond to him?

What do you remember about church today? (*Think about things like the windows, the colors, or the vestments*)

During the Offertory, gifts are presented at the altar. What special gifts will you offer this week at home, church or in school?

Mass concludes with a special blessing from the priest in order that we can glorify the Lord by our lives. In what ways were you able to do that last week?

So Say the Saints...

"Good, better, best. Never let it rest. 'Til your good is better and your better is best." ◆ *ATTRIBUTED TO ST. JEROME*

Calendar Date: _____

Church Calendar Date: _____

(i.e., 27th Sunday in Ordinary Time, Feast of Christ the King, Christmas Eve)

When Simon saw that the Spirit was conferred by the laying on of the apostles' hands, he offered them money and said, "Give me this power too, so that anyone upon whom I lay my hands may receive the Holy Spirit." ACTS 8:18-19

Which Mass did you attend today? *(Time and parish)*

Who was the main celebrant or presider? *(Name of priest who led the celebration of the Mass)*

What in particular do you remember about Mass today? *(Think about the vestment colors, readings, songs, something said during the homily)*

What did Jesus say or do in the Gospel reading today?

What about his words or actions makes you want to follow him more closely?

So Say the Saints...

"Love overcomes, love delights. Those who love the Sacred Heart of Jesus, rejoice." ◆ *ST. BERNADETTE*

Calendar Date: _____

Church Calendar Date: _____

(i.e., 27th Sunday in Ordinary Time, Feast of Christ the King, Christmas Eve)

> *And I will ask the Father, and he will give you another Advocate to be with you always, the Spirit of truth, which the world cannot accept, because it neither sees nor knows it. But you know it, because it remains with you, and will be in you. I will not leave you orphans; I will come to you.* JOHN 14:16-18

What was today's Gospel reading? *(Cite book, chapter, and verses)*

How did the Homily relate to today's readings?

During the Eucharistic Prayer we give thanks and praise to God. What are you grateful for today?

How did the songs relate to the different parts of the Mass? *(Example: Communion song was about the Body of Christ.)*

The Entrance song was about:

The song at the Presentation of the Gifts was about:

The Communion song was about:

The Dismissal song was about:

So Say the Saints...

"The feeling remains that God is on the journey, too."
◆ *ST. TERESA OF AVILA*

Calendar Date: _____

Church Calendar Date: _____

         (i.e., 27th Sunday in Ordinary Time, Feast of Christ the King, Christmas Eve)

> *The spirit of the Lord God is upon me, because the Lord has anointed me; He has sent me to bring glad tidings to the lowly, to heal the brokenhearted, To proclaim liberty to the captives and release to the prisoners, To announce a year of favor from the Lord and a day of vindication by our God, to comfort all who mourn...*   ISAIAH 61:1-2

Which Mass did you attend today? *(Time and parish)*

Other than the priest, who else processed in during the Entrance song?

Did they carry anything? What was it?

Which reading from today, including the Psalm Response, could you relate to most and why?

How did the Homily relate to things going on in your life? *(At home, at school, with friends, in the world, in your local community, at your church)*

FYI

Purgatory is a place or condition in which the souls of the just—people who have done good on earth but still need to reconcile venial sins—are cleansed, or purged of impurities. All souls in purgatory will eventually go to heaven.

Calendar Date: _____

Church Calendar Date: _____
    (i.e., 27th Sunday in Ordinary Time, Feast of Christ the King, Christmas Eve)

> John testified further, saying, "I saw the Spirit come down like a dove from the sky and remain upon him. I did not know him, but the one who sent me to baptize with water told me, 'On whomever you see the Spirit come down and remain, he is the one who will baptize with the Holy Spirit.' Now I have seen and testified that he is the Son of God." JOHN 1:32-34

What was today's Psalm Response?

In what ways can the Psalm Response help you during the week?

What was today's Gospel reading? *(Cite book, chapter, and verses)*

During the readings, including the Psalm Response, what person or thing could you identify with, and why?

What was the Recessional hymn or Closing song, and what was it about?

F Y C I

One of the oldest forms of prayer in the church is called **lectio divina.** *You use Scripture as a basis for prayer and contemplation. There are four steps:*
   1. **Choose** *a Scripture passage and read it.*
   2. **Meditate** *on its meaning to you.*
   3. **Pray** *about your response to this reading.*
   4. **Contemplate** *how God is directly communicating with you through this Scripture reading.*

Calendar Date: _____

Church Calendar Date: _____

(i.e., 27th Sunday in Ordinary Time, Feast of Christ the King, Christmas Eve)

> *For the one whom God sent speaks the words of God. He does not ration his gift of the Spirit. The Father loves the Son and has given everything over to him. Whoever believes in the Son has eternal life...* JOHN 3:34-36

What were today's first and second readings? *(Cite books, chapters, and verses)*

During the Gloria we give praise to God. In what ways will you praise God this week?

In the Prayer of the Faithful we pray specifically for our Church and her leaders, for leaders of nations and local governments, for people in need, and for things in our own families. What special intentions do you and your family have for today?

During the Gospel reading what did Jesus say or do?

How did it change the story?

How can this story from the Gospel relate to your own life?

So Say the Saints...

"Since love grows within you, so beauty grows. For love is the beauty of the soul." ◆ *ST. AUGUSTINE*

Calendar Date: _____

Church Calendar Date: _____

(i.e., 27th Sunday in Ordinary Time, Feast of Christ the King, Christmas Eve)

> *The wind blows where it wills, and you can hear the sound it makes, but you do not know where it comes from or where it goes; so it is with everyone who is born of the Spirit.* JOHN 3:8

What was today's Gospel about?

How did the people respond to Jesus?

How would you respond to him?

What do you remember about church today? *(Think about the windows, the colors, or the vestments)*

During the Offertory, gifts are presented at the altar. What special gifts will you offer this week at home, church or in school?

Mass concludes with a special blessing from the priest so that we can glorify the Lord by our lives. In what ways were you able to do that last week?

So Say the Saints...

"If God can work through me, he can work through anyone." ◆ *ST. FRANCIS OF ASSISI*

Calendar Date: _____

Church Calendar Date: _____

(i.e., 27th Sunday in Ordinary Time, Feast of Christ the King, Christmas Eve)

> Peter (said) to them, "Repent and be baptized, every one of you, in the name of Jesus Christ for the forgiveness of your sins; and you will receive the gift of the Holy Spirit. For the promise is made to you and to your children and to all those far off, whomever the Lord our God will call." ACTS 2:38-39

Which Mass did you attend today? *(Time and parish)*

Who was the main celebrant or presider? *(Priest, or leader of the celebration)*

What in particular do you remember about Mass today? *(Think about the vestment colors, readings, songs, or something said during the homily)*

What did Jesus say or do in the Gospel reading today?

What about his words or actions makes you want to follow him more closely?

_____

So Say the Saints...

"It is not hard to obey when we love the one whom we obey."   ◆ *ST. IGNATIUS OF LOYOLA*

Calendar Date: _____

Church Calendar Date: _____
(i.e., 27th Sunday in Ordinary Time, Feast of Christ the King, Christmas Eve)

> *While Peter was still speaking these things, the Holy Spirit fell upon all who were listening to the word. The circumcised believers who had accompanied Peter were astounded that the gift of the Holy Spirit should have been poured out on the Gentiles also, for they could hear them speaking in tongues and glorifying God. Then Peter responded, "Can anyone withhold the water for baptizing these people, who have received the Holy Spirit even as we have?"* ACTS 10:44-47

What was today's Gospel reading? *(Cite book, chapter, and verses)*

How did the Homily relate to today's readings?

During the Eucharistic Prayer we give thanks and praise to God. What are you grateful for today?

How did the songs relate to the different parts of the Mass?
(Example: Communion song was about the Body of Christ.)

68

The Entrance song was about:

The song at the Presentation of the Gifts was about:

The Communion song was about:

The Dismissal song was about:

So Say the Saints...

"May your creed be for you as a mirror. Look at yourself in it, to see if you believe everything you say you believe, and rejoice in your faith each day." ♦ *ST. AUGUSTINE*

Calendar Date: _____

Church Calendar Date: _____

(i.e., 27th Sunday in Ordinary Time, Feast of Christ the King, Christmas Eve)

> *But you are not in the flesh; on the contrary, you are in the spirit, if only the Spirit of God dwells in you. Whoever does not have the Spirit of Christ does not belong to him. But if Christ is in you, although the body is dead because of sin, the spirit is alive because of righteousness.* ROMANS 8:9-10

Which Mass did you attend today? *(Time and parish)*

Other than the priest, who else processed in during the Entrance song? Did they carry anything? What was it?

Which reading from today, including the Psalm Response, could you relate to most and why?

How did the Homily relate to things going on in your life? *(At home, at school, with friends, in the world, in your local community, at your church)*

So Say the Saints...

"Actions speak louder than words; let your words teach and your actions speak." ◆ *ST. ANTHONY OF PADUA*

Calendar Date: _____

Church Calendar Date: _____

Jesus returned to Galilee in the power of the Spirit, and news of him spread throughout the whole region. He taught in their synagogues and was praised by all. LUKE 4:14-15

What was today's Psalm Response?

In what ways can this help you during the week?

What was today's Gospel reading? *(Cite book, chapter, and verses)*

During the readings, including the Psalm Response, what person or thing could you identify with, and why?

What was the Recessional hymn or Closing song, and what was it about?

F Y C I

When Jesus was about twelve years old, he left his parents and went into the Temple. He stayed there for three days, preaching about God to people who were older than him. This is the first time Jesus recognized how he would serve God.

While meeting with them, he enjoined them not to depart from Jerusalem, but to wait for "the promise of the Father about which you have heard me speak; for John baptized with water, but in a few days you will be baptized with the Holy Spirit." ACTS 1:4-5

What were today's first and second readings? *(Cite books, chapters, and verses)*

During the Gloria we give praise to God. In what ways will you praise God this week?

In the Prayer of the Faithful we pray specifically for our Church and her leaders, for leaders of nations and local governments, for people in need, and for things in our own families. What special intentions do you and your family have for today?

During the Gospel reading what did Jesus say or do?

How did it change the story?

How can this story from the Gospel relate to your own life?

F Y C I

Throughout the confirmation preparation process you may hear yourself being referred to as "the confirmand," or "confirmandi." This word has its origin in Latin— confirmandus—*which means, "to be confirmed."*

Calendar Date: _____

Church Calendar Date: _____

(i.e., 27th Sunday in Ordinary Time, Feast of Christ the King, Christmas Eve)

For you did not receive a spirit of slavery to fall back into fear, but you received a spirit of adoption, through which we cry, "Abba, Father!" The Spirit itself bears witness with our spirit that we are children of God, and if children, then heirs, heirs of God and joint heirs with Christ, if only we suffer with him so that we may also be glorified with him. ROMANS 8:15-17

What was today's Gospel about?

How did the people respond to Jesus?

How would you respond to him?

What do you remember about church today? *(Think about things like the windows, the colors, or the vestments)*

During the Offertory, gifts are presented at the altar. What special gifts will you offer this week at home, church or in school?

Mass concludes with a special blessing from the priest so that we can glorify the Lord by our lives. In what ways were you able to do that last week?

So Say the Saints...

"Start by doing what's necessary; then do what's possible; and suddenly you are doing the impossible."
◆ *ST. FRANCIS OF ASSISI*

Calendar Date: _____

Church Calendar Date: _____

(i.e., 27th Sunday in Ordinary Time, Feast of Christ the King, Christmas Eve)

> *Indeed, upon my servants and my handmaids I will pour out a portion of my spirit in those days, and they shall prophesy. And I will work wonders in the heavens above and signs on the earth below.*
> ACTS 2:18-19

Which Mass did you attend today? *(Time and parish)*

Who was the main celebrant or presider? *(Name of priest who led the celebration of the Mass)*

What in particular do you remember about Mass today? *(Think about the vestment colors, readings, songs, something said during the homily)*

What did Jesus say or do in the Gospel reading today?

What about his words or actions makes you want to follow him more closely?

So Say the Saints...

"From this moment on, anything concerning me is no longer of any interest to me. I must belong entirely to God and God alone. Never to myself." ◆ *ST. BERNADETTE*

Calendar Date: _____

Church Calendar Date: _____

(i.e., 27th Sunday in Ordinary Time, Feast of Christ the King, Christmas Eve)

> *Many signs and wonders were done among the people at the hands of the apostles. They were all together in Solomon's portico. None of the others dared to join them, but the people esteemed them. Yet more than ever, believers in the Lord, great numbers of men and women, were added to them.* ACTS 5:12-14

What was today's Gospel reading? *(Cite book, chapter, and verses)*

How did the Homily relate to today's readings?

During the Eucharistic Prayer we give thanks and praise to God. What are you grateful for today?

How did the songs relate to the different parts of the Mass?
(Example: Communion song was about the Body of Christ.)

The Entrance song was about:

The song at the Presentation of the Gifts was about:

The Communion song was about:

The Dismissal song was about:

Calendar Date: _____

Church Calendar Date: _____

(i.e., 27th Sunday in Ordinary Time, Feast of Christ the King, Christmas Eve)

The spirit of the Lord shall rest upon him: a spirit of wisdom and of understanding, a spirit of counsel and of strength, a spirit of knowledge and of fear of the Lord, and his delight shall be the fear of the Lord... ISAIAH 11:2-3

Which Mass did you attend today? *(Time and parish)*

Other than the priest, who else processed in during the Entrance song?

Did they carry anything? What was it?

Which reading from today, including the Psalm Response, could you relate to most, and why?

How did the Homily relate to things going on in your life? *(At home, at school, with friends, in the world, in your community, at your church)*

F Y C I

Saint Paul, the author of many of the New Testament letters, persecuted Christians and initially denounced Jesus Christ. That changed on the day God spoke to him. Paul was instantly touched by grace and converted. He was then committed to converting and growing Christ's church.

Calendar Date: _____

Church Calendar Date: _____

(i.e., 27th Sunday in Ordinary Time, Feast of Christ the King, Christmas Eve)

No, in all these things we conquer overwhelmingly through him who loved us. For I am convinced that neither death, nor life, nor angels, nor principalities, nor present things, nor future things, nor powers, nor height, nor depth, nor any other creature will be able to separate us from the love of God in Christ Jesus our Lord. ROMANS 8:37-39

What was today's Psalm Response?

In what ways can this help you during the week?

What was today's Gospel reading? *(Cite book, chapter, and verses)*

During the readings, including the Psalm Response, what person or thing could you identify with, and why?

What was the Recessional hymn or Closing song, and what was it about?

F Y C I

The way to tell if Jesus is present in the Eucharist in a church is to find a lit candle (usually red) near the Tabernacle. When Jesus is present in a church it is customary to genuflect (go down on one knee) to show reverence.

Calendar Date: _____

Church Calendar Date: _____

(*i.e., 27th Sunday in Ordinary Time, Feast of Christ the King, Christmas Eve*)

> *Paul then said, "John baptized with a baptism of repentance, telling the people to believe in the one who was to come after him, that is, in Jesus." When they heard this, they were baptized in the name of the Lord Jesus. And when Paul laid (his) hands on them, the Holy Spirit came upon them, and they spoke in tongues and prophesied.*
> ACTS 19:4-6

What were today's first and second readings? *(Cite books, chapters, and verses)*

During the Gloria we give praise to God. In what ways will you praise God this week?

In the Prayer of the Faithful we pray specifically for our Church and her leaders, for leaders of nations and local governments, for people in need, and for things in our own families. What special intentions do you and your family have for today?

In the Gospel reading, what did Jesus say or do?

How did it change the story?

How can this story from the Gospel relate to your own life?

FYCI

The rosary helps us reflect on twenty different mysteries, or significant events, in the life of Jesus Christ.

Calendar Date: _____

Church Calendar Date: _____
(i.e., 27th Sunday in Ordinary Time, Feast of Christ the King, Christmas Eve)

...The disciples rejoiced when they saw the Lord. (Jesus) said to them again, "Peace be with you. As the Father has sent me, so I send you." And when he had said this, he breathed on them and said to them, "Receive the Holy Spirit. Whose sins you forgive are forgiven them, and whose sins you retain are retained."
JOHN 20:20-23

What was today's Gospel about?

How did the people respond to Jesus? How would you respond to him?

What do you remember about church today? *(Think about things like the windows, the colors, or the vestments)*

During the Offertory, gifts are presented at the altar. What special gifts will you offer this week at home, church or in school?

Mass concludes with a special blessing from the priest so that we can glorify the Lord by our lives. In what ways were you able to do that last week?

So Say the Saints...

"With all the strength of my soul I urge you young people to approach the Communion table as often as you can. Feed on this bread of angels whence you will draw all the energy you need to fight inner battles. Because true happiness, dear friends, does not consist in the pleasures of the world or in earthly things, but in peace of conscience, which we have only if we are pure in heart and mind." ◆ *BL. PIER GIORGIO FRASSATI*

Calendar Date: _____

Church Calendar Date: _____
(i.e., 27th Sunday in Ordinary Time, Feast of Christ the King, Christmas Eve)

And suddenly there came from the sky a noise like a strong driving wind, and it filled the entire house in which they were. Then there appeared to them tongues as of fire, which parted and came to rest on each one of them. And they were all filled with the Holy Spirit and began to speak in different tongues, as the Spirit enabled them to proclaim. ACTS 2:2-4

Which Mass did you attend today? *(Time and parish)*

Who was the main celebrant or presider? *(Name of priest who led the celebration of the Mass)*

What in particular do you remember about Mass today? *(Think about the vestment colors, readings, songs, or something said during the homily)*

What did Jesus say or do in the Gospel reading today?

What about his words or actions makes you want to follow him more closely?

So Say the Saints...

"You learn to speak by speaking, to study by studying, to run by running, to work by working, and just so, you learn to love by loving. All those who think to learn in any other way deceive themselves." ◆ *ST. FRANCIS DE SALES*

Calendar Date: _____

Church Calendar Date: _____
                  (i.e., 27th Sunday in Ordinary Time, Feast of Christ the King, Christmas Eve)

Strive eagerly for the greatest spiritual gifts. But I shall show you a still more excellent way."   1 CORINTHIANS 12:31

What was today's Gospel reading? *(Cite book, chapter, and verses)*

How did the Homily relate to today's readings?

During the Eucharistic Prayer we give thanks and praise to God. What are you grateful for today?

How did the songs relate to the different parts of the Mass? *(Example: Communion song was about the Body of Christ.)*

The Entrance song was about:

The song at the Presentation of the Gifts was about:

The Communion song was about:

The Dismissal song was about:

So Say the Saints...

"Charity is the sweet and holy bond which links the soul with its Creator: it binds God with man and man with God."   ♦ *ST. CATHERINE OF SIENA*

Calendar Date: _____

Church Calendar Date: _____
> (i.e., 27th Sunday in Ordinary Time, Feast of Christ the King, Christmas Eve)

> *...And the secrets of his heart will be disclosed, and so he will fall down and worship God, declaring, "God is really in your midst."*
> 1 CORINTHIANS 14:25

Which Mass did you attend today? *(Time and parish)*

Other than the priest, who else processed in during the Entrance song?

Did they carry anything? What was it?

Which reading from today, including the Psalm Response, could you relate to most, and why?

How did the Homily relate to things going on in your life? *(At home, at school, with friends, in the world, in your local community, at your church)*

FYCI

We must develop and maintain a moral conscience. Our conscience is the most secret core of who we are; it is the sanctuary where we meet God. In its depth we are alone with God and can hear his call to do good and avoid evil, to live as he intends for us to live. (Gaudium et Spes, Vatican Council II)

Holy Spirit, Come

Holy Spirit, come
and set upon me the fruits of your Spirit,
that I may become the hands, the feet,
and the voice of Jesus Christ in the present world.

From this moment I open my heart to you
that you may fill me with the immeasurable love of God.

By this gift, all who meet me,
whether they are lost or have not yet found their way to you,
shall come to know and love you.

Lord, my God, you have created me
uniquely in your own image that I may always know
my incomparable worth.

You took great care in giving me special gifts
to serve not only you, Lord,
but those around me.

This seal, this covenant,
this promise is for eternity.

This day I say to you, God,
"I choose, I believe, and I will honor the truth and live by it."

This journey now laid before me
may be difficult at times.

While I will try my hardest to never lose sight of you
I will rely on the Holy Spirit to guide me back should I stray.

My eternal home is with you, Lord,
and through the example of Jesus Christ your Son,
Mary the great mother of God, all the angels and saints,
as well as the faithful members of the Church
including my family and friends
who have supported me on this journey,
I know I will succeed in serving and loving you.

I will never be abandoned.

Your love is clear in the passion
and achieved in the resurrection of Jesus.

I will go forth today,
a young Confirmed Catholic,
and not be afraid to set the
world aflame with Christ's love.

Amen!

CONFIRMATION SERVICE PROJECT

Self-Accountability Record

Remember that faith and service go hand in hand. This is a record of the time you devote to service in your parish and your community.

TIME SHEET

Project: _____

Place: _____ Date: _____

Number of Hours: _____ Service Leader: _____

Signature: _____

Project: _____

Place: _____ Date: _____

Number of Hours: _____ Service Leader: _____

Signature: _____

Project: _____

Place: _____ Date: _____

Number of Hours: _____ Service Leader: _____

Signature: _____

Project: _____

Place: _____ Date: _____

Number of Hours: _____ Service Leader: _____

Signature: _____

TIME SHEET

Project: _____

Place: _____ Date: _____

Number of Hours: _____ Service Leader: _____

Signature: _____

Project: _____

Place: _____ Date: _____

Number of Hours: _____ Service Leader: _____

Signature: _____

Project: _____

Place: _____ Date: _____

Number of Hours: _____ Service Leader: _____

Signature: _____

Project: _____

Place: _____ Date: _____

Number of Hours: _____ Service Leader: _____

Signature: _____

Project: _____

Place: _____ Date: _____

Number of Hours: _____ Service Leader: _____

Signature: _____